THIS BOOK BELONGS TO:

_____

WELCOME TO LOUISIANA

Dedicated to all the explorers.

All rights reserved.
No part of this book may be reproduced in any form or by any means, electronic or mechanical, and no photocopying or recording, unless you have written permission from the author.

ISBN 978-1-958985-73-1

Text copyright © 2025 by Mimi Jones

www.joeysavestheday.com

A Mimi Book

Louisiana was named after King Louis XIV of France, a royal name for a land full of spirit.

Louisiana was the eighteenth state to join the Union. It officially joined on April 30, 1812.

Louisiana is located in the Southeastern region of the United States and is bordered by three states: Arkansas, Mississippi, and Texas.

Baton Rouge is the capital of Louisiana.
It officially became the capital in 1849.

Baton Rouge, Louisiana, has an estimated population of about 220,900 people.

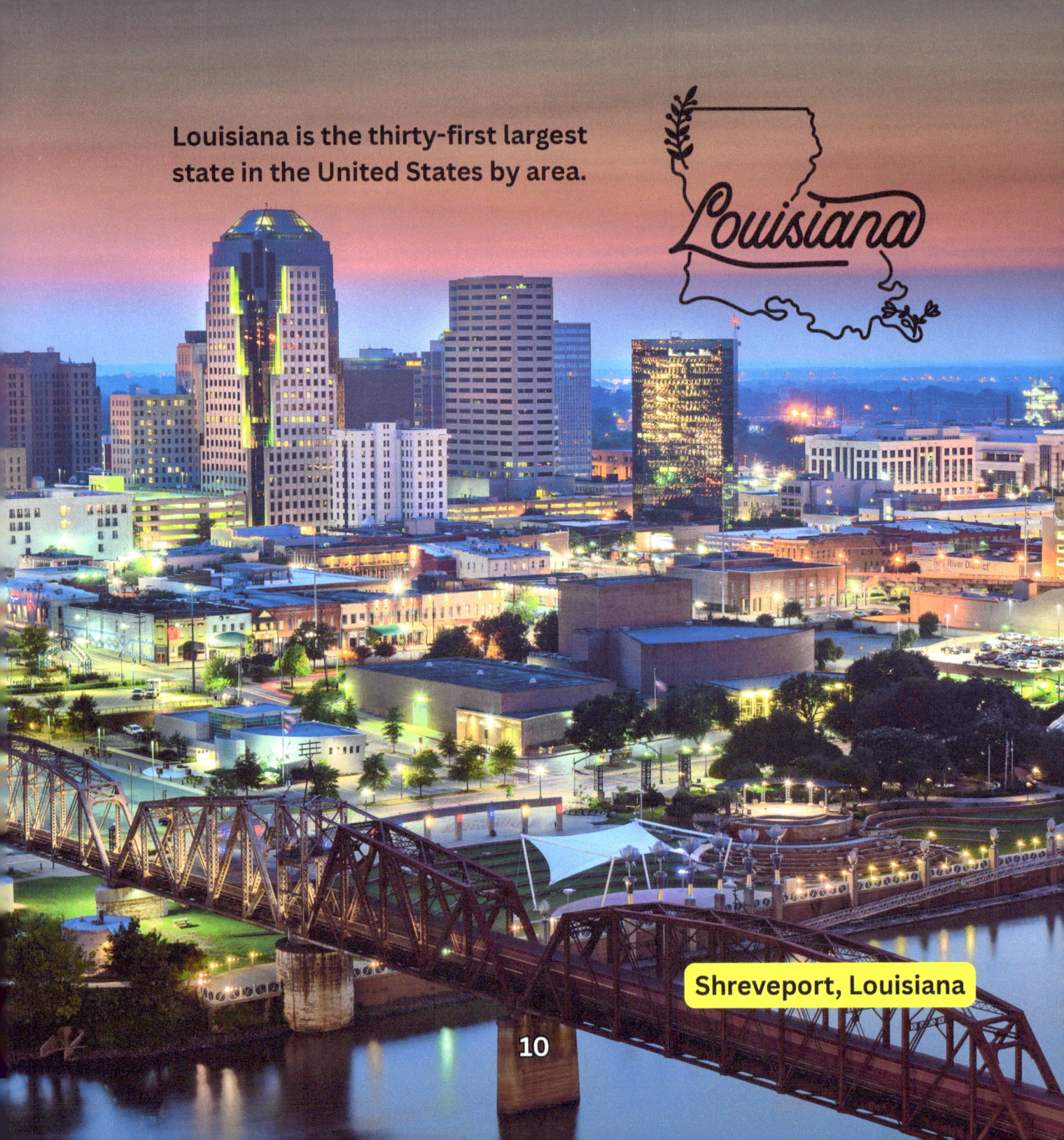

Louisiana is the thirty-first largest state in the United States by area.

Shreveport, Louisiana

There are approximately 4,657,750 people residing in the state of Louisiana.

Lafayette, Louisiana

Louis Armstrong was born in New Orleans, Louisiana. He grew up to become one of the most famous jazz musicians in the world. Louis played the trumpet like nobody else and had a voice that made people smile. His music brought joy to millions, and he helped shape the sound of jazz forever.

Crawfish are a big deal in Louisiana! These little, lobster like creatures live in the state's swamps and bayous, and they've been part of Louisiana cooking for generations. People boil them with spices, corn, and potatoes, then gather around big tables to peel and eat them by hand.

Louisiana

There are 64 parishes in Louisiana.

Here is a list of twenty of those parishes:

Ascension	Claiborne	Iberville	Orleans
Avoyelles	DeSoto	Jefferson	Plaquemines
Bienville	East Carroll	Lafourche	Red River
Calcasieu	Evangeline	Lincoln	St. Helena
Cameron	Grant	Morehouse	Vermilion

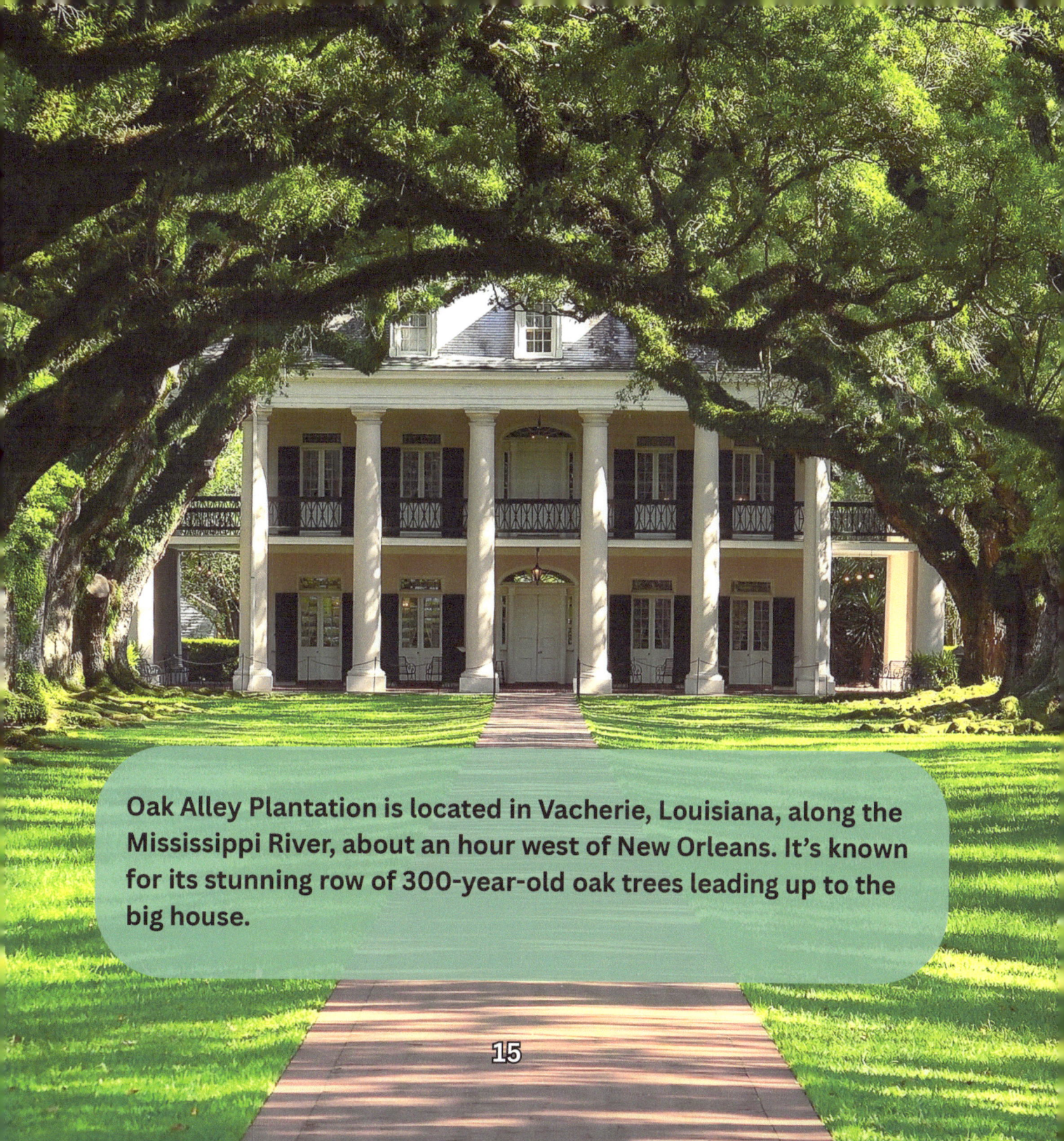

Oak Alley Plantation is located in Vacherie, Louisiana, along the Mississippi River, about an hour west of New Orleans. It's known for its stunning row of 300-year-old oak trees leading up to the big house.

Lake Martin is a peaceful lake near Breaux Bridge in southern Louisiana. Cypress trees, Spanish moss, and quiet swamp waters surround it.

Lake

The Atchafalaya Basin Bridge stretches across the swamps and bayous of southern Louisiana. Located between Baton Rouge and Lafayette, it carries Interstate 10 over the Atchafalaya Basin, the largest swamp in the United States. Built in 1973, the bridge is more than 18 miles long, making it one of the longest in the country!

Jean Lafitte National Historical Park and Preserve is located in southern Louisiana, with sites around New Orleans and the bayou country. Named after a mysterious pirate, the park protects wetlands, swamps, and cultural history.

The Louisiana state bird is the Brown Pelican. It was chosen as the state bird in 1966.

The official state flower of Louisiana is the Magnolia. It was chosen as the state flower in 1900.

Louisiana's nicknames are the Pelican State and the Bayou State.

-the-  STATE

-the-  STATE

The Louisiana state motto, "Union, Justice, and Confidence," was officially adopted in 1902.

JUSTICE

CONFIDENCE

The abbreviation for Louisiana is LA.

LA

Louisiana's state flag was officially adopted on July 1, 1912.

Some crops grown in Louisiana are cotton, corn, rice, sugar cane, sweet potatoes, and soybeans.

Some animals that live in Louisiana are alligators, beavers, deer, foxes, and squirrels.

Louisiana exhibits considerable temperature fluctuations throughout the year. The highest temperature recorded in the state reached 114 degrees Fahrenheit in Plain Dealing on August 10, 1936. In contrast, the lowest temperature, which was -16 degrees Fahrenheit (16 degrees below zero), occurred in Minden on January 19, 1994.

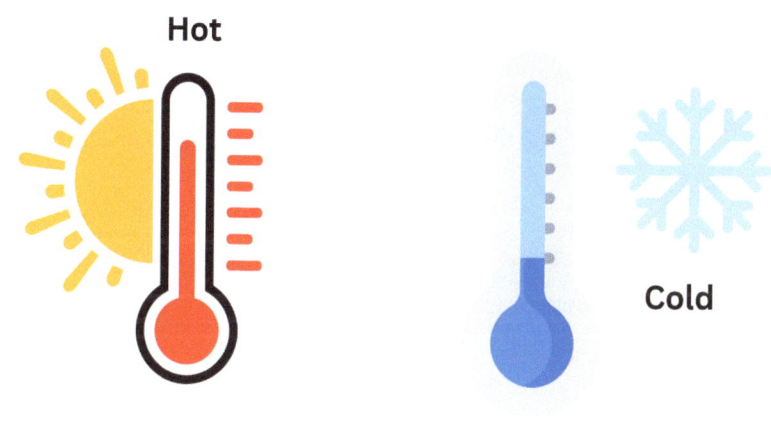

Mardi Gras

Mardi Gras is a colorful celebration held every year in Louisiana, especially in New Orleans. It takes place during Carnival season and ends on Fat Tuesday, the day before Lent begins.

LOUISIANA

The Louisiana State Museum is located in New Orleans, with several branches across the state. Its main site is located in the historic Cabildo building, adjacent to Jackson Square in the French Quarter. The museum showcases Louisiana's rich history, from Native American cultures and colonial times to jazz music and Mardi Gras traditions.

Alexandria International Airport is a welcoming travel hub located just a few miles west of downtown Alexandria, Louisiana. Nestled in the heart of Rapides Parish, this airport helps connect central Louisiana to cities across the country.

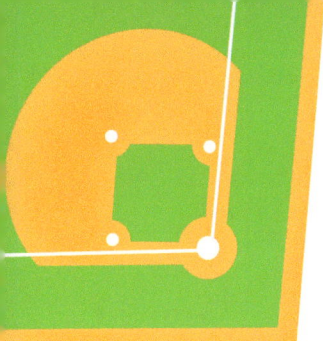

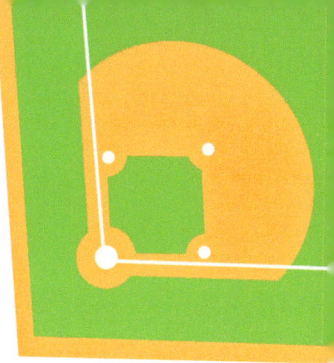

The LSU Tigers are Louisiana's proud college baseball team, based at Louisiana State University in Baton Rouge. They play at Alex Box Stadium, where fans cheer for big hits and exciting wins. The Tigers wear purple and gold and are known for being one of the best college baseball teams in the country.

FOOTBALL

The New Orleans Saints are a professional football team based in New Orleans, Louisiana. They play in the NFL and host games at the Caesars Superdome, one of the loudest stadiums in football. The team won its first Super Bowl in 2010, bringing hope and celebration to the city after Hurricane Katrina. Their colors—black and gold—shine with strength and spirit, and their symbol, the fleur-de-lis, honors Louisiana's French heritage.

LOUISIANA

Louisiana's state tree is the bald cypress, chosen in 1963. It grows in swamps and has soft needles that fall off in winter, giving it a "bald" look! Its knobby roots, called cypress knees, help it breathe in soggy soil. Strong and long-living, the bald cypress reminds us of resilience and beauty in wild places.

Louisiana is full of rivers, bayous, and salty marshes, so it has two state fish to celebrate both worlds!

• **The White Crappie**, also called Sac-au-Lait, is the freshwater state fish. It's round, silvery, and loved by families who fish in lakes and bayous.

• **The Spotted Seatrout**, or Speckled Trout, is the saltwater state fish. It's sleek and spotted, swimming in coastal waters and marshes near the Gulf.

I hope you enjoyed learning about Louisiana.

To explore fun facts about the other 49 states, visit my website at www.joeysavestheday.com. You'll also find a wide variety of homeschool resources to support joyful learning at home. If you enjoyed this book, I would be grateful if you left a review. Your feedback truly helps. Thank you for your support!

Check out these other interesting books in the 50 States Fact Books Series!

  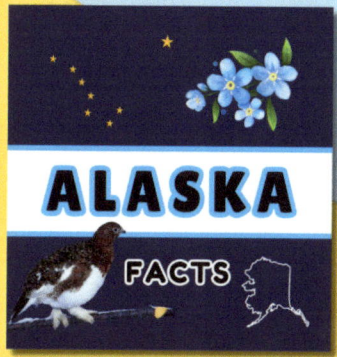

www.mimibooks.com

www.ingramcontent.com/pod-product-compliance
Lightning Source LLC
Chambersburg PA
CBHW040028050426
42453CB00002B/38